Reformed Worship

*Rightly Dividing the Word of Truth*

———•∙•∙•———

Under the series title Rightly Dividing the Word of Truth, the Reformed Free Publishing Association (RFPA) embarks on the publication of its paperback series. Based on solidly Reformed biblical exegesis and lively application of the Reformed creeds, the chapters of these volumes originally appeared as series articles in the *Standard Bearer,* the semi-monthly periodical also published by the RFPA. The goal of publishing this series is to give broader life to the subjects as originally treated by the *Standard Bearer* editorial staff. The RFPA initially intends to make two volumes available per year on a variety of timely topics.

Books in this series include:

David J. Engelsma, *Common Grace Revisited*
David J. Engelsma, Barry Gritters, Charles Terpstra, *Reformed Worship*
Herman Veldman, *The Providence of God*

Additional titles are under consideration.

# Reformed Worship

David J. Engelsma, Barry Gritters,
and Charles Terpstra

Reformed Free Publishing Association
Grandville, Michigan

For information, contact:
Reformed Free Publishing Association
4949 Ivanrest Ave SW
Grandville, MI 49418-9709
Phone:    (616) 224-1518
Fax:       (616) 224-1517
Website: www.rfpa.org
E-mail:   mail@rfpa.org

ISBN 0-916206-83-1
LCCN 2004092484

# Contents

# Preface

———•·•·•———

Because the Protestant Reformed Churches earnestly want to be obedient to Jesus Christ in their public worship, they look both ways more than once before they cross into a new neighborhood of worship practices. They feel very safe (that is, humbly obedient to Jesus Christ) in their old neighborhood.

The reason for this is not that they want to be stuffy traditionalists. Rather, the Protestant Reformed Churches desire to be obedient to Jesus Christ. They are opposed to the modern forms of worship because they believe them to be disobedience to Jesus Christ. If worship were a matter of personal preference, no critique of modern worship would be permitted. Since Christ regulates worship, Christ requires us, and will help us, to judge all forms of worship.

Contemporary worship, as opposed to traditional worship, is all the rage. Go into most religious bookstores and you will not miss the wall of glitzy-covered books explaining and defending this new way of worshiping God. Some of them are intelligent, articulate, and scholarly. Others are less reasoned, but more impassioned defenses. The authors are all sure of one thing. God likes what they are doing.

Convinced that God is pleased with what the Protestant Reformed Churches are doing in worship, we give our voice to a defense of Reformed, biblical, covenantal worship. Let us not call it traditional. Let us call it Reformed, biblical, covenantal worship. And let us analyze the admittedly new forms of worship in the light of Scripture, by which everything must be tested.

The form and manner of our worship of God is no light matter. In his treatise, *The Necessity of Reforming the Church,*

John Calvin made this judgment of the importance of proper worship:

> If it be asked, then, by what things chiefly the Christian religion has a standing existence amongst us, and maintains its truth, it will be found that the following two not only occupy the principal place, but comprehend under them all the other parts, and consequently *the whole substance of Christianity,* viz., a knowledge first, of the right way to worship God; and secondly of the source from which salvation is to be sought. When these are kept out of view, though we may glory in the name of Christians, our profession is empty and vain.[1]

By saying this, Calvin not only asserts that one cannot be a Christian without a proper knowledge of worship, but he ranks the importance of the knowledge of proper worship higher than the knowledge of salvation by grace alone through faith alone and Christ alone! (See also his *Institutes:* II.8.11)

Again, according to Calvin, the Christian's primary duty is to maintain pure worship.

> There is nothing to which all men should pay more attention, nothing in which God wishes us to exhibit a more intense eagerness than in endeavoring that the glory of his name may remain undiminished, his kingdom be advanced, and the pure doctrine, which alone can guide us to true worship, flourish in full strength.[2]

Here, Calvin shows his opinion of the proper relation between pure doctrine and proper worship: "Pure doctrine...guide[s] us to true worship." Doctrine is worship's servant.

Calvin is not mistaken in his assessment of the importance of worship. The reason for our very existence, in time and

---

1. Quoted in Carlos Eire, *War Against the Idols: the Reformation of Worship from Erasmus to Calvin* (Cambridge: Cambridge University Press, 1986), 198.
2. Ibid., 199.

eternity, is to bring worship to our great and good redeemer God in Jesus Christ. God requires his people to bring him united praise. Bodies of believers in local congregations assemble on the special day of worship to give honor to their Lord.

Both the Old Testament and the New Testament record the primary place of the worship of God by God's redeemed people. Psalm 122:1 reflects the believer's attitude to this requirement of God: "I was glad when they said unto me, Let us go into the house of the LORD." He sings: "With joy and gladness in my soul I hear the call to prayer; let us go up to God's own house and bow before Him there."[3] This call to worship was echoed in Psalm 95:6: "O come, let us worship and bow down: let us kneel before the LORD our maker."

The new covenant church joyfully carries on this calling. It's a good thing we can do it with joy, because that is what we will be busy with in God's eternal kingdom—worshiping God! "And I saw another angel fly in the midst of heaven, having the everlasting gospel to preach unto them that dwell on the earth, and to every nation, and kindred, and tongue, and people, saying with a loud voice, Fear God, and give glory to him; for the hour of his judgment is come: and worship him that made heaven, and earth, and the sea, and the fountains of waters" (Rev. 14:6,7; see also Rev. 22:8,9). The everlasting gospel is: "Worship God."

BARRY GRITTERS
Professor of New Testament and Practical Theology
Theological School of the Protestant Reformed Churches

---

3. Psalter number 348 in *The Psalter with Doctrinal Standards, Liturgy, Church Order, and Added Chorale Section.* Rev. ed., (PRC) (Grand Rapids, Mich.: Eerdmans Publishing Co., 1998).

# 1

# The Regulative Principle of Worship

*David J. Engelsma*

———◆·◆·◆———

ONE OF THE MOST POWERFUL WINDS BLOWING THROUGH
the Reformed and Presbyterian churches today is the hurri-
cane of "liturgical renewal," or "progressive worship." The
service of public worship as the Reformed have conducted it
for hundreds of years is summarily scrapped as "traditional"
("traditional" being uttered with scorn or with sorrow, as
though describing a service that was either foolish or useless).
The traditional service is replaced with a service of bands and
singing troops; banners; films, skits, and drama; dialogues;
dancing; and shallow, man-centered, Arminian, but lively
"gospel songs."

Often the two kinds of services are placed back-to-back on
a Sunday morning. The traditional service is at 9 A.M.; the
progressive service is at 11 A.M. Every member can indulge his
preference.

The assumption of those who spend their waking hours
planning the demolition of the traditional Reformed worship
and concocting new and more appealing activities of worship
is that the church is free to shape the worship of God as she
thinks best. And what she thinks is best is whatever pleases the
worshiping people.

This assumption is shared by most of the "conservative"
members of the churches where progressive worship is introduced. They dislike the innovations intensely. They com-

1

plain. They attend only the 9 A.M., traditional service. But they tolerate the new worship.

*How* we worship is a matter of preference.

*Our* preference.

## Definition

This assumption is shattered on the rock of the regulative principle of worship. The regulative principle of worship is that God himself regulates, or rules, the public worship of himself by his church. God regulates worship by clearly prescribing in his Word what this worship must consist of. God himself tells us *how* to worship him. This *how* refers to the inner, spiritual disposition of the worshipers: "in spirit and in truth" (John 4:24). It also refers to the elements of the service of worship: the preaching of the gospel; the two sacraments, rightly administered; prayers and congregational singing; and the offerings, especially for the poor.

God does not leave the *how* of worship to the wisdom and whim of the worshiping people. It is not even the case that God permits the church to worship him in any way that she sees fit, as long as nothing in the worship obviously conflicts with his Word. Often Reformed people will defend some aspect of worship by saying, "It is not forbidden by Scripture." This is the Lutheran and Anglican position on worship: whatever is not forbidden is permitted.

The distinctively Reformed position is radically different: whatever is not *prescribed* is forbidden.

## Public Worship

This principle of public worship is in accord with the nature and purpose of worship. Public worship is the fellowship of God with his people in the covenant of grace; God meets with his people in the Word and Spirit of Jesus Christ. In this meeting, God prescribes the manner of the meeting, not we. He is sovereign, stipulating the *how* of worship, just as he stipulates who is to be worshiped.

Public worship has as its purpose the praise of God, not the religious satisfaction of those who worship. And God determines how he is to be praised.

As regards the benefit of worship for God's people, this benefit is edification. It is not spiritual entertainment, emotional excitement, aesthetic titillation, and the like. And God prescribes, because he alone knows, the content of worship that will build up the saints.

God, who knows us and who knows the rulers of the church, would never leave such an important activity as worship to our discretion. Foolish, sinful people will soon invent a worship more to their own liking—worship that is not centered in, based on, and permeated with the Word; worship that is not theocentric; worship consisting of ceremony and ritual; worship that is more conformable to contemporary culture; worship that caters more to ourselves.

Rulers of the church who have the authority to legislate worship, rather than to minister and administer God's regulations, will do exactly what rulers began to do very early in the history of the church. This resulted in the impressive, but empty and abominable service of Rome. And, in fact, the movement of "progressive worship" and "liturgical renewal" is leading Reformed and Presbyterian churches back to Rome.

## Progressive Worship

Progressive worship is revolution against the regulative principle of worship, that is, revolution against the authority of God in the sphere of worship. I do not refer to this or that outrageously offensive aspect of progressive worship, whether a dramatic portrayal of the crucifixion or a liturgical dance, but progressive worship *as such* rebels against divine regulation of the service by Holy Scripture. It shapes the service according to what seems fitting, moving, and effective to the worship leader or to the people themselves.

What drives the new worship? "I like it!" "We feel that this or that religious activity would be a nice addition to the service!" "We were moved by it!" "This will draw the people, especially the young people!" The decisive question is, "What pleases the people?" We can put it this way: Man's own will governs the worship. The Bible calls this worship "will-worship" (Col. 2:23).

We should not underestimate the power of the movement of progressive worship. It is in large part the reason why Willow Creek Community Church in the Chicago area, Calvary Church in Grand Rapids, and hosts of similar churches throughout North America are booming. They cater to the preferences of the people. This is their strategy.

The true church may expect, perhaps is already experiencing, pressure to "learn" from the new worship, always "within limits," of course. This will come from the carnal members on her rolls and from the carnal natures of the living members.

Against the incoming tide stands the regulative principle: *God's* wishes decide the worship. Our wishes have as little to do with the *how* of worship as they do with *whom* we worship. How the church worships is not a matter of our preference. It is a matter of God's command.

It is discouraging then that reputedly conservative men in the Reformed and Presbyterian churches deny and even attack the regulative principle. Rev. Steve Schlissel is busy doing this. He has written a series of articles entitled, "All I Really Need to Know about Worship...I Don't Learn from the Regulative Principle."[1]

Although he pays lip service to the regulative principle, the Presbyterian theologian John Frame, in fact, empties it of any governing power over the worship services he leads and the

---

1. *Messiah's Mandate*, 1999.

worship services of anyone who heeds his instruction on worship. "It is virtually impossible to prove that anything is divinely required specifically for official services."[2]

Frame, supposedly a conservative at a reputedly conservative seminary, enthusiastically promotes the contemporary, progressive worship that is destroying the traditional Reformed worship regulated by God's Word. Frame approves teaching in the services of public worship by people who are not elders; children's church; drama as a legitimate form of preaching; teaching by means of dialogue; infant communion; worship services that are entirely given over to music, that is, services without any Bible reading or preaching; and liturgical dance.

This is to repudiate the regulative principle by gutting it and to substitute for it, as the rule for worship, the fancies of modern Presbyterians and the tastes of worship leader John Frame. Showing which way the wind is blowing, the book comes highly recommended by four leading Presbyterian theologians at two leading, purportedly conservative Reformed seminaries.

No one who fears God will say that the whole matter is unimportant. The right worship of himself by his chosen people is God's ultimate purpose in creating and redeeming them. "This people have I formed for myself; they shall shew forth my praise" (Isa. 43:21).

Such is the importance of the right worship of God by the church that God has devoted the entire first table of the law to it. The first commandment prescribes *whom* we must worship. The third prescribes *wherein* we must worship him. The fourth prescribes *when* we must worship him.

And the second?

The second prescribes *how* we are to worship God.

God thinks that the important question about the manner of the worship of his people is, "What pleases him?"

So do we.

---

2. *Worship in Spirit and Truth* (Phillipsburg, NJ: P&R Publishing, 1996), 44.

# 2

# The Basis of the Regulative Principle of Worship

*David J. Engelsma*

———•◦•———

## Biblical Basis

THE REGULATIVE PRINCIPLE IS BIBLICAL. IT IS THE truth about worship laid down in the second commandment of the law of God: "Thou shalt not make unto thee any graven image, or any likeness of any thing that is in heaven above, or that is in the earth beneath, or that is in the water under the earth: Thou shalt not bow down thyself to them, nor serve them..." (Exod. 20: 4, 5a). The second commandment differs from the first in that the first prescribes the *object* of our worship—*whom* we are to worship, whereas the second prescribes the *manner* of our worship—*how* we are to worship.

When God forbids us to worship him by means of images, he forbids us to worship him in any way whatsoever of our own devising. Forbidding improper ways of worship, he teaches, positively, that his Israel must worship him only in the way that he prescribes in Holy Scripture.

This teaching, which is the heart of the second commandment, is the regulative principle of worship.

Clearly implied in the second commandment are the two great characteristics of pure worship of the God of Israel and the church. The first is that right, pure worship is spiritual.

The condemnation of images has its source in the spirituality of the being of God. As spirit, God requires spiritual worship.

The new, contemporary, progressive worship conflicts with this characteristic of pure worship. It is nothing but a plethora of outward ceremonies and rituals.

The second characteristic of right worship implied by the second commandment is that it is a service of the Word: the Word *read,* the Word *preached,* the Word *sung,* the Word *prayed,* and the Word *signified and sealed.* The Heidelberg Catechism teaches this in Question 98. Explaining the second commandment, the Catechism declares that God will have his people taught, and thus himself worshiped, "not by dumb images, but by the lively preaching of His Word."[1]

The new worship fights against this characteristic of pure worship. The effect of every form of contemporary worship, if not the avowed purpose, is to marginalize the Word, to give less and less time and prominence to the reading and preaching of the Word, and, finally, to drive the Word out of the service altogether. It is not unheard of by this time, in Reformed and Presbyterian churches, that the service on Sunday evening is totally devoid of the preaching of the Word. There is not even the perfunctory nod toward preaching of the customary 10- or 15-minute homily. Reformed theologians, including reputedly conservative Reformed theologians, are now openly defending worship services in which the preaching of the Word has no place.

## Confessional Basis

There can be no challenge by Reformed persons to the interpretation of the second commandment as laying down the regulative principle of worship, for this is the explanation of the Reformed confessions. For those whose creeds are the

---

1. Heidelberg Catechism, in vol. 3 of *Creeds of Christendom,* ed. Philip Schaff (Grand Rapids, Mich.: Baker Book House, 1998), 343.

Three Forms of Unity, Question and Answer 96 of the Heidelberg Catechism is authoritative. To the question, "What does God require in the second commandment?" the Catechism answers: "That we in nowise make any image of God, nor worship him in any other way than he has commanded in his Word."[2]

Stated positively, the Catechism here teaches that we must worship God only in the way that he has commanded in his Word. And this, for the Catechism, is the requirement of the second commandment.

The Belgic Confession also teaches that our worship is strictly controlled by the will of Christ in Scripture. Although the subject is the government of the church by the elders, the Confession declares: "We reject all human inventions, and all laws which man would introduce into the worship of God, thereby to bind and compel the conscience in any manner whatever."[3]

The Westminster Confession of Faith binds the regulative principle on all Presbyterians:

> But the acceptable way of worshiping the true God is instituted by himself, and so limited to his own revealed will, that he may not be worshiped according to the imaginations and devices of men ... or any other way not prescribed in the Holy Scripture.[4]

Accepting and practicing the regulative principle is confessional for Reformed and Presbyterian churches and people. Rejection of the regulative principle is attack upon the confessions. For an office bearer this is transgression of his sacred vow to maintain and defend the confessions.

---

2. The Heidelberg Catechism, in *Creeds of Christendom*, 343.

3. The Belgic Confession of Faith, Article 32, in *Creeds of Christendom*, 423.

4. The Westminster Confession of Faith, 21.2, in *Creeds of Christendom*, 646.

## Traditional Basis

Recognition and spirited defense of the regulative principle also has solid support in the Reformed tradition. I choose three worthy representatives. None of these was a Puritan or a Scottish Presbyterian. This is not to say that a Scottish Presbyterian would not be a worthy representative of the tradition, only that he would not speak so convincingly to the readers.

In his commentary on the Heidelberg Catechism, Zacharias Ursinus explains the second commandment as requiring "such worship...as is pleasing to him, and not with such worship as that which is according to the imagination and device of man...a rule [is] given," Ursinus continues, "that we sacredly and conscientiously keep ourselves within the bounds which God has prescribed, and that we do not add anything to that worship which has been divinely instituted, or corrupt it in any part, even the most unimportant."

He continues, "To worship God truly is to worship him *in the manner which he himself has prescribed in his Word*" (emphasis added).[5]

About a hundred years later, the renowned Gijsbert Voetius, delegate to the Synod of Dordt and champion of the Reformed faith, taught the same. Voetius wrote a commentary on the Heidelberg Catechism in question and answer form. Treating the Heidelberg Catechism's explanation of the second commandment, Voetius asked when it happens that men worship in violation of the second commandment. His answer was:

> Whenever one wills to honor and serve [God] by means of images, or whenever one wills to worship Him in such a manner as directly conflicts with God's Word *or that is apart from God's Word*, founded on the institutions of man, or on our own whims and

---

5. Zacharias Ursinus, *Commentary on the Heidelberg Catechism* (Phillipsburg, NJ: Presbyterian and Reformed Publishing Company, 1852), 517.

fancies, as takes place under that of the papacy by means of its ceremonies and human traditions.[6]

Voetius then asks, "What is here [in the second commandment] commanded us?" His answer is: "That we must worship God according to the regulation of his Word."[7] To the question of whether we may use such ceremonies as Rome has, Voetius answers no, because "all such ceremonies are *self-willed and arbitrary* worship, contrary to Matthew 15:9, Galatians 1:8, and Colossians 2:18" (emphasis added).[8] These are the texts to which the Reformed tradition has always appealed in support of the regulative principle. Matthew 15:9 is Jesus' warning, "But in vain they do worship me, teaching for doctrines the commandments of men."

In their defense of the regulative principle, both Ursinus and Voetius show themselves faithful disciples of John Calvin, who is the third representative of the Reformed tradition.

I marvel at the audacity, or ignorance, of the Reformed theologians and ministers today who dismiss the regulative principle and open up Reformed worship to the self-willed, arbitrary, and fanciful ceremonies that characterize progressive worship. Either they do not know, or do not care, that Calvin taught the regulative principle. Either they do not know, or do not care, that Calvin urged the regulative principle as essential to right, Reformed religion because he saw that rejection of the regulative principle was in large part the cause of Roman Catholic superstition and idolatry.

Calvin's commentaries on the prophets are full of his impassioned warnings to the Reformation churches to practice and uphold the regulative principle of worship. Commenting on Amos 5:26, Calvin writes:

---

6. Gijsbert Voetius, *Voetius' Catechisatie over den Heidelbergschen Catechismus* (Rotterdam: Gebroeders Huge, 1891), 783. My translation from the Dutch.

7. Ibid., 784.

8. Ibid., 797.

We ought not to bring any thing of our own when we worship God, but we ought to depend always on the word of his mouth, and to obey what he has commanded...when men dare to do this or that without God's command, it is nothing else but abomination before him.[9]

Explaining Isaiah 57:6, Calvin says:

The Jews chose their own method of worshipping God, and turned aside from the rule which he had laid down in his Law; and consequently...every kind of worship which they followed by their own choice was abominable and wicked; for in religion and in the worship of God it is only to the voice of God that we ought to listen.[10]

Finally, I refer to the commentary that Calvin was working on at his death, the Ezekiel commentary. This is Calvin's comment on Ezekiel 20:28:

Not only does God wish worship to be offered to himself alone, but that it should be without any dependence on human will: he wishes the law to be the single rule of true worship; and thus he rejects all fictitious rites... *It is in [God's] power to determine how he ought to be worshipped;* and when men claim this power to themselves, it is like ascending to the very throne of God (emphasis added).[11]

The regulative principle of worship is Reformed, confessional, and biblical. We may and must worship God *only* as he prescribes in his Word. This worship is accepted by him. Tra-

---

9. John Calvin, *Commentaries on the Twelve Minor Prophets: Joel, Amos, Obadiah,* tr. John Owen, vol. 2 (Grand Rapids, Mich.: Baker Book House, 1998), 298.

10. John Calvin, *Commentary on the Book of the Prophet Isaiah,* tr. William Pringle, vol. 3 (Grand Rapids, Mich.: Baker Book House, 1998), 202.

11. John Calvin, *Commentaries on the First Twenty Chapters of the Book of the Prophet Ezekiel,* tr. Thomas Myers, vol. 2 (Grand Rapids, Mich.: Baker Book House, 1998), 320.

ditional Reformed worship is scorned by the "worship leaders" and shunned by the worshiping multitudes today. But one thing may be said in its favor, and we are bold by the grace of God to say it: It pleases God.

*Only* this worship pleases God.

Progressive worship is praised to the skies today, and the people throng the courts of religious entertainment where actors act, dialogists dialogue, musicians make music, movie makers show movies, dancers dance, and the congregation sings mindless fundamentalist ditties and rank Arminian heresies. But one thing must be said against it, and we are bold by the grace of God to say it: It displeases God.

It is image worship.

# 3

# The Regulative Principle of Worship Applied

*David J. Engelsma*

———•••———

Reformed believers and churches may not differ as to the fact and importance of the regulative principle of worship. As the preceding chapter demonstrated, the regulative principle is confessional. The importance of the regulative principle, according to the confessions, is nothing less than this; it is the truth of the second commandment of the law.

Difference among Reformed and Presbyterian Christians and churches has to do with the *functioning* of the principle in the worship service. The difference can be divisive.

The question is: How does the rule that God determines the manner of worship *apply* to the public worship of the church?

Misunderstanding of the application of the regulative principle, on the part of some of its most ardent advocates, is responsible for a great deal of the division between Reformed and Presbyterian churches which are, in fact, one in the gospel of sovereign grace.

## Elements of Worship

Generally, the regulative principle applies to the *content,* or *elements,* of the public service of worship. The function of the regulative principle is to prescribe the *elements* of the public worship of the church. The regulative principle limits the church to these prescribed spiritual activities as the means of communing with God, praising God, and being edified ourselves.

What these elements are, the Reformed and Presbyterian churches have known ever since the Reformation. Both of these ecclesiastical sisters have made these elements a matter of confession in their official creeds. The Reformed have done this in Question and Answer 103 of the Heidelberg Catechism. The Presbyterians have done the same in Chapter 21 of the Westminster Confession of Faith.

According to Question and Answer 103 of the Catechism, in which the Catechism is explaining the fourth commandment, Scripture prescribes as the elements of the only worship that is pleasing to God the following: the reading and preaching of the Word; administration of the sacraments; prayers and singing; and offerings, particularly for the poor.

> Q. What does God require in the fourth commandment?
> A. In the first place, that the ministry of the Gospel and schools be maintained; and that I, especially on the day of rest, diligently attend church, to learn the Word of God, to use the holy Sacraments, to call publicly upon the Lord, and to give Christian alms. In the second place, that all the days of my life I rest from my evil works, allow the Lord to work in me by his Spirit, and thus begin in this life the everlasting Sabbath.[1]

No other activity is permitted. Whatever is not commanded is forbidden.

The regulative principle does not stipulate that there must be an express biblical command for everything that goes on in a worship service. Such things may include what the minister wears; whether to stand or sit to pray and sing; how the bread and wine of the Lord's Supper are distributed; whether the singing is accompanied by an organ, begun with a pitchpipe, or led by a precentor; and the like.

---

1. The Heidelberg Catechism, in *Creeds of Christendom*, 345.

Some zealots like to present the regulative principle as requiring biblical warrant for every detail of a worship service, but this is to mistake the principle. The southern Presbyterian worthy John Girardeau was guilty of this error. His is the dubious honor of having authored what may be the most violent assault upon instrumental accompaniment of congregational singing ever launched. He called the accompaniment of congregational singing by an organ or piano "heresy in the sphere of worship."[2] But Girardeau brought instrumental accompaniment under the condemnation of the regulative principle by misstating the principle. He described the regulative principle this way: "Whatsoever, *in connection with* the public worship of the church, is not commanded by Christ...in his Word, is forbidden" (emphasis added).[3]

In fact, the church has liberty "in connection with public worship" to arrange a great many details of her worship: what time she meets; how often the Supper is administered, and how; the order of worship; sitting or standing for prayers and songs; form prayers used in administering the sacraments and in exercising discipline; instrumental accompaniment of the singing; and more.

There are *circumstances* attending worship as well as the elements themselves, and one reduces the regulative principle to an unworkable principle, if not to absurdity, if he attempts to apply it to every detail of worship. The New Testament church has liberty in Christ to arrange the details of her worship, and this liberty is important. The Belgic Confession of Faith claims this liberty for the Reformed church. In the context of the worship of God, the Confession states that "it is useful and beneficial that those who are rulers of the Church institute and establish certain ordinances among themselves for maintaining the body of the Church."[4]

---

2. John L. Girardeau, *Instrumental Music in Public Worship* (Barkeyville, PA: New Covenant Publication Society, 1983), 179.

3. Ibid., 200.

4. The Belgic Confession of Faith, Article 32, in *Creeds of Christendom,* 423.

Can we agree that the *elements* of worship are regulated by express command of Christ in Scripture? And can we agree what these elements *are?* If so, we are a long way toward oneness in worship, and we ought to be encouraged to pursue oneness of mind on the differences that remain.

Let us bravely consider certain of these differences regarding worship that divide Reformed and Presbyterian churches which are truly one in the gospel of grace.

## Instrumental Accompaniment

Instrumental accompaniment of the singing of the congregation is not an element of worship. The element of worship is the singing of the congregation. Instrumental accompaniment is merely an attending *circumstance* intended to serve the singing of the congregation. The regulative principle is completely uninterested in instrumental accompaniment, and has nothing to say about it. The church has liberty here. She is free to use an organ or piano; she is free to get started singing by means of the twanging of a pitch-pipe; she is free to have a strong-voiced precentor lead the singing; she is free to sing without any accompaniment.

The second commandment has as little to do with instrumental accompaniment as it does with the means by which the deacons take the offerings, whether by a plate or by a bag or even by a box in the corner with a hole in the top.

If only the instrument serves the singing of the congregation!

## Forms and Formulas

Then there is the matter of occasional use of form (as opposed to free) prayers, the reading of the law, and the congregation's confession of her faith by means of the Apostles' Creed. These are legitimate aspects of the elements of worship that God prescribes. God requires prayers. Some may well be form prayers. Some can *better* be form prayers. The prayers that are part of the administration of the sacraments and of the exercise of excommunication, precisely declaring the doctrine and exactly spelling out the application to the lives of the people, should not be left to the phraseology of the individual minister. The Lord's Prayer is a form prayer. The important thing about the prayers offered at church is that they display the "requisites" of those prayers that are acceptable to God and that he will hear (see the Heidelberg Catechism, Q & A 117).

God requires the reading of Scripture. The law is part of Scripture. Reading the law every Lord's Day is proper under the regulative principle, to say nothing of the benefit of doing so.

God requires praise, including confession of his truth. Reciting the Apostles' Creed is such confession. Reciting the Apostles' Creed is proper under the regulative principle, to say nothing of the benefit of doing so.

## Observance of Christmas

Some Presbyterian advocates of the regulative principle vehemently denounce Reformed churches for observing Good Friday, Easter, Ascension Day, Pentecost, and Christmas with special worship services. Such observance is alleged to be violation of the regulative principle. Their argument is that God has not commanded the church to worship on April 21 or December 25 in observance of Good Friday or Christmas. In reality, they charge Article 67 of the Church Order of Dordt and thus the synod of Dordt and the entire Dutch Reformed tradition with image worship.

The charge rests on a misunderstanding of the regulative principle. The regulative principle prescribes the *content* of the public worship, not the *time* when the church worships. It is the fourth commandment that prescribes the *time* of public worship. And, although the fourth commandment insists that the church worship on the Sabbath Day, it permits the church to worship also on other days. The Heidelberg Catechism explains the fourth commandment this way: "...that I, *especially* on the day of rest, diligently attend church" (emphasis added).[5]

In the heyday of the Reformation, there were preaching services virtually every day of the week. As regards the Reformed church's observance of the great events in the ministry of Christ, one of the earliest and most respected Reformed creeds, the Second Helvetic Confession (1566)—not a Dutch creed!—explicitly approved it, "*highly,*" as an aspect of the church's "liberty":

> Moreover, if in Christian liberty the churches religiously celebrate the memory of the Lord's nativity, circumcision, passion, resurrection, and of his ascension into heaven, and the sending of the Holy Spirit upon his disciples, we approve of it highly.[6]

One may like Dordt's rule in Article 67, or one may dislike it, but observance of Christmas and the other "Christian festivals" has absolutely nothing to do with the regulative principle whatever. What the regulative principle requires is this: *If* you have a service of worship to remember Jesus' birth on December 25, this service must consist of the same elements as the worship on Sunday. The special Christmas service must consist of preaching, praying, congregational singing, and giving of alms. It may not take the form of dramatic presentations of the manger scene, liturgical dance, instruction by means of banners, and the like.

I plead with our Presbyterian brothers and sisters not to find differences that divide where none exist.

The purpose of looking at these controversial matters is to plead that such differences in applying the regulative princi-

---

5. In *Creeds of Christendom*, Q&A 103, 345.

6. *Reformed Confessions of the 16ᵗʰ Century*, ed. Arthur C. Cochrane (Philadelphia: The Westminster Press, 1966), 292.

ple do not betray fundamental disagreement over the regulative principle itself. Thus, it is hoped, this examination of differing application of the regulative principle will make for peace among those who are truly one in ecclesiastical subjection to the second commandment.

# 4

## The Regulative Principle of
## Worship and Singing

*David J. Engelsma*

———— •:•:• ————

### The Songs at Church

THE QUESTION IS THIS: DOES THE REGULATIVE PRINCIPLE
demand exclusive Psalmody, or does it allow for hymns? By
*hymns* I refer to songs which, although biblical, are not based
on the Psalms.

Some Presbyterian and Reformed churches argue for exclusive Psalmody as the requirement of the regulative principle. This implies the judgment that the singing of a hymn in
a worship service, whether it is the doxology, "Praise God
from Whom All Blessings Flow," or the Lord's Prayer, is transgression of the second commandment. Obviously, this position makes close ecumenical relations with churches that sing
any hymns impossible.

The Protestant Reformed Churches are a Psalm-singing
denomination. Singing the Psalms has been an important
part of their heritage from the very beginning of their existence some 75 years ago. They maintain this part of their
heritage without change to the present moment. The Protestant Reformed Churches sing only the Psalms in worship
with the exception of a few specified hymns. What the
churches sing in worship is governed by Article 69 of their
church order:

> In the churches only the 150 Psalms of David, the Ten Commandments, the Lord's Prayer, the Twelve Articles of Faith, the Songs of Mary, Zacharias, and Simeon, the Morning and Evening Hymns, and the Hymn of Prayer before the sermon shall be sung.[1]

Of these nine hymns, five are never sung, most of them being unknown to the people. In addition to singing some of these hymns infrequently, all of the churches sing "Praise God from Whom All Blessings Flow" as the opening doxology at every service, and one or two sing the hymn, "May the Grace of Christ our Savior," as a closing doxology on occasion.

The Protestant Reformed Churches are Psalm-singing churches. Hymns have almost no place in the services.

## Reasons for Singing the Psalms

The Protestant Reformed Churches are Psalm-singing churches not because they believe exclusive Psalmody is the requirement of the regulative principle. Obviously not! No church that thinks that the regulative principle demands exclusive Psalmody will permit any hymn to be sung ever at worship. The article that rules the singing in worship of this church will read: "In the church only the 150 Psalms of David shall be sung." Period!

There are other reasons than the regulative principle for singing the Psalms at church, virtually exclusively. From 1959 to 1962, the Protestant Reformed Churches considered becoming a hymn-singing denomination. The occasion was an overture from one of the churches to the synod of 1959 to change Article 69 of the church order to include many more hymns. In response to this overture, the synod of 1960 moved

---

1. *The Church Order of the Protestant Reformed Churches and Constitutions of Standing Synodical Committees, Rules and Regulations, Formulas, By-laws.* Revised and updated. n.p.: Synod of the Protestant Reformed Churches in America, 2002.

to change Article 69 to read: "In the churches only the 150 Psalms of David shall be sung, *as also such Hymns which are faithful versifications of the Holy Scriptures,* in each case the General Synod being the judge" (emphasis added).[2] This motion was not then adopted, but was referred back to committee for further study. The result was a lively debate in the churches until 1962 when the issue was finally decided by the synod. The debate was carried on in the *Standard Bearer,* in private discussions, and annually at the synods of 1961 and 1962. The conclusion was a decision by the synod of 1962 defeating the motion to open up the worship services to hymns.

The significant thing about the debate is that neither the friends nor the foes of hymns in worship argued on the basis of the regulative principle. The regulative principle simply did not figure in the discussion. Although the decision by the synod of 1962 included no grounds for the defeat of the motion to make the Protestant Reformed Churches a hymn-singing denomination (which is highly regrettable, since the issue was both important and controversial), the decision was certainly not grounded in the regulative principle.

The reasons why the Protestant Reformed Churches sing Psalms in worship (and the reasons, presumably, why the synod of 1962 defeated the motion to introduce hymns) include the greater spirituality of the Psalms, especially their God-centeredness; the fact that the Spirit has given the church one songbook—the Psalms—by inspiration; the danger that the inclusion of hymns will soon drive the Psalms out of the worship of the church altogether; and the lesson of history that good hymns are invariably followed by a host of corrupt hymns—songs that are superficial, songs that are centered on man and his religious feelings, and songs that are Arminian.

This last was in the mind of George Ophoff when he commented on Article 69 of the church order in his notes on "Church Polity":

---

2. *Acts of Synod and Yearbook of the Protestant Reformed Churches in America, 1960,* 115, 116.

> The lesson of history is that when a group of Reformed churches begin to apostatize from the truth of God's Word, they also begin introducing the hymns for liturgical purposes. Let us never, as a communion of churches, substitute hymns for the 150 Psalms of David.[3]

In their stand that Reformed churches should sing the Psalms in worship, virtually exclusively, but on other grounds than that the regulative principle requires exclusive Psalmody, the Protestant Reformed Churches perfectly represent and carry on the tradition of the Dutch Reformed Churches. The Synod of Dordt decided on Psalm-singing, in part because the Arminians were urging the introduction of hymns into the worship of the Reformed churches in the Netherlands. The Arminians intended to have their heresy sung into the minds of the people. But Dordt did not ground this decision in the regulative principle and, therefore, Dordt permitted a few, specified hymns. The reason why Dordt mentioned these hymns was that they were part of the songbook in use at the time and were popular with the people. Nevertheless, Dordt could permit them, which a synod holding to exclusive Psalmody as a requirement of the regulative principle could not have done.

Abraham Kuyper acknowledged the attempt by some members of the Dutch Reformed churches to make exclusive Psalmody a matter of the regulative principle. But the real reasons for their attempt were practical. These members saw and feared the harmful consequences of introducing hymns into the churches' songbook.

Kuyper listed six reasons why the Dutch Reformed, in the days of their spiritual strength, insisted on remaining Psalm-singing churches and rejected hymns in the public worship.

1. Holy Scripture presents us with a special volume of Psalms [for singing].

---

3. George M. Ophoff, "Church Polity" (notes, library of David J. Engelsma, n.d.), 152.

2. The Psalms far exceed hymns in depth of spirituality.
3. Hymns have rarely forced their way into the churches without soon revealing the tendency first to dominate the Psalms and then to oppose them.
4. In the Psalms is heard the abiding, eternal keynote of the godly mind, while all hymns mostly convey a temporary theme and impress the one-sided conception of the moment upon the churches.
5. Hymns invariably have led to choirs [in public worship], by which the congregation was silenced.
6. In the struggle between hymns and Psalms, the careless and weaker [Dutch: *onverschilligen*] members of the congregation all sided against the Psalms and for hymns, while the godly always chose more for Psalms against hymns.[4]

To these six reasons should be added another. The lesson of history is that the introductions of hymns into the worship services has always opened the way for the churches to sing heretical hymns, particularly Arminian hymns about a universal grace of God.

Kuyper spoke of the "preference" of the Reformed churches for Psalm-singing in public worship because of the "abuse" to which the introduction of hymns invariably has led.[5]

Kuyper demonstrated that the position that exclusive Psalmody is required by the regulative principle is untenable, but he agreed that the Reformed churches should remain Psalm-singing churches on the practical grounds that have always weighed heavily with Reformed believers. Kuyper was especially impressed with the argument that wherever hymns were introduced, "the hymns stole the heart [of the congregations], and the heart was estranged from the Psalms."[6]

The conclusion of the Dutch theologian and churchman

---

4. Abraham Kuyper, *Onze Eeredienst* (*Our Public Worship*) (Kampen: Kok, 1911), 56. My translation from the Dutch.

5. Ibid., 57.

6. Ibid., 60.

was that the Psalms should continue to function as "the main constituent of our liturgical singing."[7] The Reformed churches "ought to remain conscious of this, without scrupulosity or exaggeration."[8] By adding *without scrupulosity or exaggeration,* Kuyper warned the churches not to make exclusive Psalmody a matter of the regulative principle. *Scrupulosity* would condemn singing the doxology "Praise God from Whom All Blessings Flow," the Lord's Prayer, the Apostles' Creed, or the "Song of Mary," as violation of the second commandment.

Kuyper called the Reformed churches to remain standing exactly where Article 69 of the Church Order of Dordt places them. Kuyper was right.

In the main, these reasons for singing Psalms and for keeping hymns out of the service were the "conclusions" of the study committee that reported to the Protestant Reformed synod of 1960. It was a puzzling move of that committee, on the basis of a report and "conclusions" that were overwhelmingly opposed to the introduction of hymns nevertheless to recommend that synod decide to open up public worship in the Protestant Reformed Churches to the singing of hymns (see *Acts of Synod, 1960,* pp. 115, 116). The "conclusions" really called for synod to *reject* the overture to introduce hymns. And that is what the synod of 1962 rightly and wisely did.

The churches ought resolutely to maintain their Psalm-singing position, on the grounds that have prevailed in the Reformed churches of the Dutch tradition.

In terms of the regulative principle, which does, of course, govern our singing at church, the stand of the Protestant Reformed Churches is this: God requires the congregation to sing, and he requires the congregation to sing *his Word;* the soundest and safest and perfectly adequate policy is to sing his Word as found in the Psalms, which is, after all, the songbook that God has given us.

No one should suppose that this stand implies blanket re-

---

7. Ibid., 61.
8. Ibid., 61.

jection of hymns. With the Psalms, we sing good hymns in our homes, in our choral societies and programs, and in our schools. Yes, also in our schools. We expect that the schools will teach the children to love and sing the Psalms. The Psalms should even have pride of place in the singing at school and in the singing by the school. But there must not be a reactionary insistence that the schools sing only the Psalms. There are many God-glorifying and edifying songs in addition to the Psalms that the people of God may sing themselves and enjoy. Handel's *Messiah* comes immediately to mind, and Toplady's "Rock of Ages," and the great trinitarian hymn of the early church, "Glory be to the Father." Neither the regulative principle nor deep piety has a word to say against our use and enjoyment of such music in our personal, family, and social life.

## The Importance of the Regulative Principle

The regulative principle governs the content, or elements, of the public worship of the instituted church.

This principle is important.

First, it safeguards our worship. How important this is in our day, when many of the churches are swept away in the movement of "liturgical renewal." All worship that originates in men's thinking, what Colossians 2:23 calls "will-worship," is cursed of God. The second commandment itself makes plain how serious it is to ignore the regulative principle: God is a jealous God. Reformed and Presbyterian churches must take this warning seriously.

However, a church's holding to the regulative principle does not automatically guarantee acceptable worship. The church must *practice* her worship "in spirit and in truth." Also, there are Presbyterian and Reformed churches that are zealous for the regulative principle, exceedingly zealous, so that they enforce not only the principle but also their own application of the principle to indifferent circumstances. But these same churches preach a gospel of universal, resistible grace, which is the dishonoring of worship at its very heart.

Nevertheless, the regulative principle is important to keep the worship of the true church pure.

Second, the regulative principle enables the worshiping people of God to be sure that their worship pleases God and is edifying to themselves. The question arises at church: Does this please God? Inasmuch as we only do what he himself prescribes, we can be sure of it.

On the other hand, the progressive crowd, amid their banners, dances, choirs, dramas, dialogues, and musical troupes, are subject to dreadful uncertainty: "All this pleases the professional worship leaders, but does it please God?"

Third, the regulative principle maintains the unity of the church. All of the members are bound to one and the same mode of worship. It is not that of the older or of the younger. It is not that of the educated or of the uneducated. It is not that of the white or of the black. It is not that of the "conservatives" or of the "liberals." It is God's way of worship—for old and young; for educated and uneducated; for whites and blacks; for "conservatives" and "liberals."

Abandonment of the regulative principle brings about division. Ask the members of the churches where it is thrown out.

Fourth, the regulative principle in the confession and practice of the churches glorifies God. God is glorified by the solemn, simple, Word-centered, and Word-based worship prescribed by the regulative principle. He is also glorified in this, that he—*he!*—determines how he will be worshiped.

The regulative principle is the application to worship of the Reformed church's confession, "Let God be God!"

# 5

## Contemporary Worship Practices

*Barry Gritters*

————•·•·•————

### What Is Contemporary Worship?

THERE ARE THREE MAIN KINDS OF CONTEMPORARY WOR-
ship. Each goes off in a different direction, but all go away
from Reformed, biblical, covenantal worship.

First, there is the loose, unplanned, uncontrolled, wild
worship of the charismatics. It has foot stomping and hand
clapping, waving of arms and swaying of bodies, speaking in
tongues and healing of sick and paralyzed, falling on the
floors and, sometimes, uncontrolled laughter. Included in
these services is almost always drama and contemporary (or
more accurately, "rock with a band") music.

Second, there is the relatively new "seeker-service," carefully crafted to appeal to the baby boomer generation and the
unchurched. The service is determinedly casual, includes
contemporary music and, usually, drama-plays.

Third, there is the "High-Church," or "liturgical" service of
some Reformed and Presbyterian churches. *Liturgical* is a
word that simply means *service*. It is used in Scripture to describe the work of the priests in the temple. Today, it refers to
the elements of our worship. Historically, it has described a
kind of service that emphasizes ceremony and solemnity. This
is the worship of the Roman Catholics and the Anglicans. The
new liturgical services are also characterized by much formal
ceremony. They have banners and pictures (projected or

28

hung), clerical robes, gowns, and candles. Symbolism is emphasized. These services also generally include drama-plays, sometimes with contemporary music.

These three cannot be lumped into one category for analysis, nor does a particular service necessarily have only the elements of one kind of service; some have an eclectic taste. But three elements appear in almost all of them: dance (in one way or another), rock music (some kind of modern music), and drama-plays.

We are concerned primarily with the seeker-services and the liturgical services, not because the charismatic service is not an error, but because it is not as immediate a threat to the Reformed faith.

## The Seeker-Services

By *seeker-service* is meant a service of worship designed to appeal to those who are probably not members of any church, but are *seeking* something in a church, or perhaps are even *seeking* God.

These services can be identified by what they *do not* want as much as by what they *do* want. They do not want anything that sounds or looks "churchy." They do not want a typical church building style. They do not want a pulpit from which something is declared to them. They do not want an organ. They do not want old songs. They assuredly do not want formal dress.

The visitor must feel comfortable. He is not accustomed to church. The whole atmosphere must be normal, natural, and pleasant.

In order to create an atmosphere as un-churchlike as possible, they want a theater-like building. They often want lights—percussive lights, colored lights, all kinds of lights sweeping the audience. They call for guitars—usually amplified, loud, electric guitars playing rock music or country, if not hip-hop and pop. The assembled multitude is "warmed up" by the praise band for 45 minutes or so. Then the worship leader (notice he is not called a preacher) takes his place on his stool and begins his chat. There are banners, pictures, and video-projectors. Casual dress—blue jeans and tennis shoes—is the dress code in some places.

For all their differences, these seeker-services have in common that there is little preaching. Emphasis falls on the aesthetic—what pleases and attracts the eye.

The people of God should not be naïve regarding the popularity of the seeker-service. The young people must be informed of them. Pastors and elders, but especially parents, must show that the present worship of God in the congregations pleases him. But most important is the need that in our worship services the young people and adults worship the Lord in the beauty of holiness and find all their needs met in the simple, unadorned gospel of Jesus Christ and him crucified.

## The Liturgical Service

The second type of innovation in modern worship is the liturgical service. There is much ceremony, formalism, and a robed clergy, as though you were in an Anglican or Roman Catholic Church. There is much more to this second type, though, than the formalities of Rome and Canterbury.

For examples of this kind of service, I read articles in *Reformed Worship* magazines, most of which are not recognizably Reformed.

In one sample service proposed for use, children dressed up to be Bishop Ambrose of Milan, Martin Luther, John Calvin, and others. Each actor began by saying, "Good evening, my name is..." Then they recited a little history of the person, explained why he wrote the hymn he did, and asked the congregation to sing the hymn. This was meant to be the substance of the worship service.[1]

---

1. Randall D. Engle, "Songwriters tell their Stories," *Reformed Worship* (Dec., 1999): 36–39.

Another local church had "Picture Jesus" as the theme for the weeks of Lent. Their banners, bulletin covers, and projected pictures all were intended to help worshipers "study the character of their Savior more closely" with "a gallery in which a variety of portraits were displayed... to illustrate the multiple dimensions of the person and work of Jesus."[2]

One suggestion for worship during advent was to hang large figures of angels over the windows of the sanctuary, one more each week and increasing in size toward the front. The purpose was to "fill the worship space with angels so that as they heralded Christ's birth on Christmas morning, the effect would hint at the overwhelming announcement to the shepherds."[3] Then, members of the congregation carried forward in procession copper flames matching those carried by the angels. Why the emphasis on angels? The "growing popularity of angels among believers and unbelievers alike provided an opportunity to intersect the message of salvation with popular culture."[4]

In another article, it was suggested that the congregation celebrate an Old Testament Seder meal (part of the Passover feast) during worship. The author presented elaborate descriptions of the different elements of the meal and how to participate in this feast. Aside from the decidedly Jewish and pre-Christian slant to this suggestion, the justification for the practice is that "it is important for us to acknowledge the problems and injustices of our times, but we must have hope that things are not inalterable."[5] Not one word about the gospel and the cross of Christ. Not one mention of sin, our real bondage.

Pray that the Lord will spare your church from such folly.

---

2. Howard Vanderwell and Norma deWaal Malefyt, "Picture Jesus," *Reformed Worship* (Dec., 1999): 10–19.

3. Timothy Van Zalen, "The Cross meets the Video Projector," *Reformed Worship* (Sept., 1999): 12.

4. Ibid.

5. Diane Quaintance, "Learning About the Seder Meal," *Reformed Worship* (Dec., 1999): 20.

It is the sin of "will-worship" as Paul describes it in Colossians 2:23. Its origins are not the Scriptures. What no confessing Christian would dare claim for his *individual* service of God, many boldly proceed to do in their *public* service: "*I* will decide for myself how to serve God."

But "will-worship" is our sin, always. Our nature inclines us to the same, always. Privately and publicly, we want to determine for ourselves how to serve God.

Pray that the Lord will spare us, personally, from the desires of our own heart and give us a heart after his heart, for his glory, into eternity. Practice well. Eternity is a long time.

## The Defense of the Innovations

But the modern forms of worship are not without their own defense. Realizing that what they are doing is new, the proponents of contemporary worship at least attempt a defense of their practices.

From a practical standpoint, their defense is that the church must reach the unchurched. They ask the question: "What will make the unchurched comfortable enough to lure him into the sanctuary?" They often find an answer. A local newspaper report covering a new mega-church showed a young man (one of the 5,000 who attends regularly) in jeans, tennis shoes, and a sweatshirt, proclaiming: "This makes me feel good; I'm comfortable here; that's why I'm here." Good feelings have become the standard, rather than a search for the truth.

Proponents of contemporary worship seek worship that applies to our particular circumstances, worship that is applicable and relevant to our age. The worship must appeal to baby-boomers, "Generation Xers," and those who have little ability or interest to read or think linearly. Because we live in an electronic, image-oriented age, they feel that they must use electronics and images that people are familiar and comfortable with.

As Andy Langford puts it, "Western society was turning away from the printed word and bound texts, toward an audio and video culture."[6] Therefore, he believes, churches need to find direction for worship in "our recent culture. Fresh cultural realities, new musical expressions, changing aesthetic values, and new styles of personal expression *demanded a fundamental reevaluation of received worship traditions.*" Thus the "advent of radically contrasting new styles of worship ... to meet these modern realities."[7]

The pastor of one local mega-church explains: "We are trapped in an evangelical sub-culture ... we are isolated in our own *little* world. That world is basically out of touch with the broader culture."[8] He believes that the church must "place the gospel in a culturally relevant context."[9]

The blurb on a book from a "reformed" author defending the innovations says that the author "offers us what we need most right now—biblical principles of worship that we must apply to our particular circumstances."[10] What it ought to say is: "With an eye on modern culture, the author mutilates Reformed worship to fit the Procrustean bed of modern culture."

The theological defense of proponents of contemporary worship is the incarnation and the need to think and act "incarnationally."

Their reference to incarnation, of course, is to the reality that God became man in Jesus Christ. Their appeal is to John 1:14: "And the Word was made flesh, and dwelt among us." Their interpretation of this passage is that Christ accommo-

6. Andy Langford, *Transitions in Worship: Moving from Traditional to Contemporary* (Nashville: Abingdon Press, 1999), 41.

7. Ibid., 38.

8. Ed Dobson, *Starting a Seeker-Sensitive Service: How Traditional Churches Can Reach the Unchurched* (Grand Rapids, Mich.: Zondervan Publishing House, 1993), 114.

9. Ibid., 16.

10. Richard L. Pratt, Jr., review of *Worship in Spirit and Truth,* by John M. Frame.

dated himself to the particular culture and age when he was born and lived with the Jews.

They believe that Christians must "be incarnational" in the way Jesus was. "The Incarnation—God taking human form—witnesses to God's affirmation of humanity in a particular cultural context. Jesus, the Word become flesh, preached inside and outside of the synagogue and temple and took the gospel to a lake, mountainsides, homes, and streets. Peter invited Gentiles into the church, and Philip witnessed in a chariot to an Ethiopian eunuch."[11]

This author means that Christians must live in the neighborhood with the styles of the neighborhood. The neighborhood doesn't understand our music, so we must use theirs. They think that Christians must contort themselves to fit the mold of the neighborhood. In dress, in language, in music, the church must become like the world.

The church must not conform to the world. Let the church call sinners to conform to the church, and to the beauties of her Lord, Jesus Christ.

---

11. Langford, *Transitions in Worship,* 69.

# 6

# A Reformed Critique of Contemporary Worship

*Barry Gritters*

————•·•·•————

THE PROTESTANT REFORMED CHURCHES AGREE WITH Carlos Eire in his contention that "the rebellion of man in regard to worship displeases God tremendously, not only because of the act of disobedience, but because of the form of worship it creates. It is insult added to injury."[1] Perhaps Eire could have said, "Injury added to insult." For first, this rebellion insults God by worshiping without regard to his commands; then it injures God by creating a form of worship that disfigures and deforms both him and his church.

We believe that since worship is the primary calling of God's people, both now and eternally (see Revelation 14:6,7; 22:9), it is not possible to exercise too much carefulness in determining our manner of worship.

The Heidelberg Catechism explains God's requirement in the second commandment of God's law: "that we in nowise make any image of God, *nor worship him in any other way than he has commanded in his Word*" (emphasis added).[2]

---

1. *War Against the Idols: the Reformation of Worship from Erasmus to Calvin* (Cambridge: Cambridge University Press, 1986), 206.
    2. The Heidelberg Catechism, in *Creeds of Christendom*, Q&A 96, 343.

## A Reformed Critique

These modern worshipers have no biblical warrant for what they do. Their worship committees are not governed by the "regulative principle of worship," that is, the principle according to which the form and content of worship must be regulated strictly by the word of God. These worship trail-blazers do not go to Scripture with their questions. They go to culture, to the neighborhood, or to the community.

Because of this, they ask the wrong questions. The question is not "How does the neighborhood behave?" The proper, God-honoring questions are, "What does God in his Word require us to do when we gather for his praise? How must we behave in his presence?" Thus, they end with a multitude of difficulties and errors.

First, they are inevitably man-centered, not God-centered. Because they ask, "What is the neighborhood like?" they craft their services after man's desires. They are committed to the idea that we go to the place of worship to get something *from* God, rather than to bring something *to* God. The question is not "What makes us feel good?" but rather, "Of what worship is this great and glorious God worthy?"

Because these worship services are man-centered, they are "performance-oriented." Whether it's the high-powered Robert Schuller's invitation to Tommy Lasorda to tell the people of the Crystal Cathedral how the "Great Dodger in the Sky" helped him to win games and lose weight, the local talent in the praise band, or the adolescents in the drama, it is performance-oriented.

They are walking, if not running, back to the same unbiblical practices that the Reformers condemned so vehemently in the Roman Catholic Church when worship was done for the people.

In that connection, a second error of the new worship services is that they take away from the congregational and covenantal aspect of worship. They are individualistic. The people don't praise together, but watch others praise. A Reformed worship service is marked by the deliberate desire to have all the people participate in everything they possibly can.

A third error is that these contemporary services do not distinguish between mission work and worship. Mission work and trying to preach to unbelievers is one thing. Public worship is quite another. Those who advocate contemporary worship, appealing to the example of Jesus on the seaside and Philip in a chariot, are making a simple but fundamental mistake; they confuse evangelism with public worship of the gathered people of God.

The result is that the unchurched who have come to a church of this style now have formed a judgment of what worship is. And these "seekers" who have found it are not led to a biblical, reverent way of approaching God. They are still worshiping like the neighborhood. Instead of transforming the world by the renewing of their minds, the church is allowing itself to be "conformed to the world" (Rom. 12:2).

A fourth error is that these services inevitably take away from a sense of the awesome majesty of God.

For them, God is cool, probably a kindly, gray-haired old man who winks at everyone and judges no one. He is easygoing and probably a lot like us. There is no reverence, no sense of awe, not even in the liturgical services with all the pomp and ceremony, because the attention is on the players.

Though God in Christ is our Friend, to whom we may come close and with boldness, he is still God! He is and always will be the awesome figure of Revelation 1: 14–17a; "His head and his hairs were white like wool, as white as snow; and his eyes were as a flame of fire; And his feet like unto fine brass, as if they burned in a furnace; and his voice as the sound of many waters. And he had in his right hand seven stars: and out of his mouth went a sharp two-edged sword: and his countenance was as the sun shineth in his strength. And when I saw him, I fell at his feet as dead." That's the awesome glory of the God whom we worship.

The worship God delights in is the kind the four beasts and twenty-four elders of Revelation 4:8b, 10-11 give to God: "...and they rest not day and night, saying, Holy, holy, holy,

Lord God Almighty, which was, and is, and is to come . . . The four and twenty elders fall down before him that sat on the throne, and worship him that liveth for ever and ever, and cast their crowns before the throne, saying, Thou art worthy, O Lord, to receive glory and honour and power: for thou hast created all things, and for thy pleasure they are and were created."

Because a wrong conception of God is conveyed in these services, everything is crooked. Whatever the delivered message says, the whole service conveys the wrong message, an unbiblical one. These unchurched visitors learn about the "new faith." A visitor to these new worship services gets the impression that the Christian faith is primarily about self— making *me* feel good, helping *me* be a good person, and getting what *I* want from God. They do not get the correct understanding that the Christian faith is about *God*—knowledge of the holy God through his word, sorrow for sin against him, and the sacrifice of self to serve others for his sake.

A fifth error is that these services detract from the preached Word. It matters not which kind of contemporary service it is, or what the motives are, the end result is that there is usually no time for the preaching. If there is time, the minister sits on the pulpit in a casual manner, submitting to the people some of the thoughts he has come up with through the past week.

The preaching in its saving, comforting power is absent. Preaching as the voice of Jesus Christ himself is gone.

Just as serious, the preaching in its judging, condemning power has disappeared. We may not forget this in our analysis of contemporary worship. In very nature and purpose— to be user-friendly, attractive, appealing, non-confrontational, inoffensive—contemporary worship's preaching cannot be antithetical. Sharp warnings, calls to repentance, threats of eternal judgment for impenitent sinners, even shutting the gates of the kingdom for some, is necessarily absent.

# 7

## Proper Worship

*Barry Gritters*

•◆•

IN CONTRAST TO THE NEW FORMS OF WORSHIP, WHAT IS proper worship? Reformed, biblical worship is *covenantal*. Protestant Reformed worship is certainly not contemporary. But neither is it simply traditional. Traditional can mean a lot of things. Even *reformed* does not mean much today, although our worship is certainly reformed if it is anything. But I prefer not to describe it now as simply reformed, or even biblical, although it is both.

Our worship—proper, God-glorifying worship—is also *covenantal*. By that, I mean that our worship emphasizes, is enjoyment in, and is a celebration of, the gracious union of friendship between God and his people in Jesus Christ. The covenant itself is the experience of friendship.

### Covenantal Worship

Covenantal worship, then, is simply (profoundly!) the experience of God "tenting" with us ( John 1:14) in Jesus Christ, through the only thing we glory in—the cross of the Lord Jesus Christ. The Friend of his people comes to them closely, lovingly, intimately, for mutual delight and God's glory. Little is more important and mutually delightful to a Christian husband and wife than a loving, close, intimate relationship. So a Reformed believer views worship of his God.

As covenantal, this worship centers in the Word. The worship will have at its heart the word of God preached, sung, prayed, confessed, and believed. Every kind of worship that takes away from the Word is a service that undermines the great reality and exquisite delight of God's friendship with his people.

The Word serves the covenant in three ways.

First, the Word serves God's gracious covenant in that, by the preaching of the gospel, God gathers his covenant people to himself.

Because the preaching is what it is—the powerful voice of God himself through a man called by the church—the preaching alone has the power to bring men and women out of darkness into the great light of his presence (Rom. 1:16; 1 Cor. 1:18-24; 1 Thess. 2:13).

Preaching creates, out of nothing, life in men as really as the voice of God in creation brought forth plants and animals out of nothing. Preaching raises from the dead as really as the voice of Jesus Christ brought Lazarus from the grave. When it does that, those raised from the dead and given life come to God as his friends! Worship is drawing nigh unto God. Since no one can come unto Christ, except the Father who sent Christ draws him, the Father irresistibly draws by the preached Word (John 6:44).

Worship services that do not have preaching are worship services that do not make Christians. They may make members, or followers of some minister, but they do not make Christians!

Because God's covenant also includes children, the covenant requires that we take children to worship services as soon as they are able to sit still and be quiet. We do not have children's church, sending out the children under a certain age to sit in another room to color pictures. We certainly do not have children's church where someone sits on the podium with the children in a circle telling a little story for the entertainment of the indulgent parents who smile and whisper politely to each other.

"Oh, we have children's church," I always tell questioners.

We have it during the week when the children of different age groups gather to hear the preaching of the gospel to them in *catechism*. Every Monday evening for the teenagers, every Wednesday afternoon for the children, we have "children's church," if you want to call it that—worship designed for the age level of the children. At the same time, God's children learn very early to listen to the preaching with the assistance of their faithful parents. In an amazing way, the Holy Spirit provides them their "milk" of the gospel, while their parents enjoy meat (1 Pet. 2:2).

A second way in which the preaching of the word serves the covenant is that, by preaching, the covenant of God and the God of the covenant are glorified.

When the word is preached as it ought to be preached, the great work of God to establish his friendship with his people is proclaimed. God's people need and want to hear that good-news proclamation. Preaching declares to the church that the great Creator of heaven and earth determined to be a friend with sinners. Preaching declares that the glorious covenant God came to live with sinners in the incarnation—that is the significance of John 1:14: "And the Word was made flesh, and dwelt among us: (and we beheld his glory, the glory as of the only begotten of the Father,) full of grace and truth." But because a holy God does not fellowship with unholy people ("follow . . . holiness, without which no man shall see the Lord" Heb. 12:14), preaching declares that the covenant Son of God laid down his life as satisfaction of the justice of God, so that the barrier of sin between him and us could be removed. Oh, the glorious work of God to establish his covenant with us! And, because the covenant God is a faithful God, preaching declares that he will never forsake his covenant friends.

These things are preached. Week after week these things are preached, so that the people of God may know the goodness of the God who is their Friend.

The third way in which preaching serves the covenant is that in preaching, God actually engages in covenant life with his people.

Preaching is the actual fellowship of God with his blood-bought, eternally chosen children. In preaching, God speaks to us in fellowship, as his friends. He speaks tenderly, graciously, and personally to the hearts of his people. Christ said, "the words that I speak unto you, they are spirit, and they are life" (John 6:63).

But why preaching, ultimately? Why always the Word? Could not God have fellowshipped with his people in some other way? Why not in plays, with drama? Why not with rock music? Why not with dances and banners and bands?

Because God's own covenant life within himself is a life of fellowship in the Word! Eternally, God enjoyed communion with himself by the Word and Spirit. What is Jesus Christ, but the eternal "WORD"? Think of God's eternal life within himself as a sweet communion of conversation through the Word and Spirit. By his Word and Spirit, God is close to himself, shares his own covenant life within himself, and delights in himself.

We read in 1 Corinthians: "It pleased God by the foolishness of preaching to save them that believe" (v. 21). To save by preaching is God's eternal decree. But it is no cold, hard, meaningless decree. It is his pleasure—the exquisite good pleasure of God, because it shows his own active covenant life within himself.

This is the heart of our criticism of any kind of contemporary worship that takes away from the preaching: it leads the people away from a true knowledge of God in himself.

## Lessons to be Learned

Is there nothing to be learned from contemporary worship? Indeed, but not what might be expected.

First, we learn how idolatrous our natures are. We are all attracted to the visible, the sensational, the easy, and the casual. We are idolaters in our nature.

Second, we should learn to be careful not to overreact to

the chaos and anarchy of the charismatic worship, or the loose and casual worship of the mega-churches, so that we are tempted to embrace the liturgical formalism and pomp of Eastern Orthodoxy or Rome. There is no small temptation for people to do that. Hundreds are flocking back to the majesty and dignity and sense of reverence in Rome.

Third, let us learn to be fervent to bring the gospel in evangelism and personal witnessing to those who would never darken the door of a church. One of the criticisms of Reformed worshipers is that they are not interested in evangelism. Of all people in the world, we Reformed ought to be most zealous in bringing the gospel to the ends of the world and to our next-door neighbor who would never come into our church building.

Fourth, let us be careful to worship in Spirit and in truth. One criticism of traditional worship is that it is staid, formal, cold, and lifeless. But the new worship services are lively, spiritual, happy, loud thanksgivings to Jehovah God. Is that true? Is traditional worship not heart-felt, lively, and spiritual? Does your minister not speak to the heart of Jerusalem? Does his preaching not speak to your emotions as well as your intellect?

This is no little danger for us. It is unbiblical to say that worship is primarily for the intellect (unless by that is meant that the intellect is to be addressed first, and not only or mainly).

Finally, we are reminded that we live in a radically wicked, swiftly changing world, where people think differently than a generation ago, where people don't read and think, but watch and feel. Ours is a generation of electronics, of images, of videos and computers and entertainment. It is one of the most difficult ages in which to be faithful in serving God that has ever been. This is the world our children are growing up in.

How will we teach them? What will we say to them? Must we change the way we worship? God forbid. By the grace of God we will continue to teach them to read, to think, to reason, to meditate on the precious word of God in Jesus Christ.

And we will remind them with personal, experiential joy, that the everlasting gospel is this: Worship God in Spirit, and in truth.

# 8

## The Active Participation of Believers

*Charles Terpstra*

———— •◦• ————

THE TOPIC BEFORE US MAY SEEM TO BE ONE THAT IS relatively simple and clear, even free of any controversy. Who would possibly dispute that the believer is to be an active participant in the public worship of God? And who would argue what the believer ought to be doing in the worship service, namely, praising and thanking God through singing, hearing the Word, prayer, and giving?

But the fact is that this subject is worthy of special and separate treatment. This is true for several reasons.

For one thing, criticism has been made regarding the believer's role in what is called traditional worship services. The criticism is that the believer's role is too passive and insignificant. The pastors and elders are the only leaders and are therefore the only ones really involved in the worship service. They get to do things, while the Christian in the pew just sits there, passively watching things happen. The regular church member does not have an active role in this type of service.

In response to this, the contemporary church has opened up the worship services to more lay-member involvement. There are worship teams, made up of members who plan and prepare and lead the services. Young people are being asked to lead services. Children are being given a more visible role in certain services. This is the trend because that has been the criticism. We want to address that criticism and that trend.

But there is another reason why this subject deserves to be treated. There is a real danger that we, too, not only *think* the same way, namely, that our role is entirely passive, but also *act* this way in the worship of God. That is, the danger is present that we are not truly active in our worship, but just show up and let things happen. We may go through the motions so that we are active but not in the right way. We may participate, but not consciously and fervently and gratefully—so that we are not thinking about what we are doing and why and for whom.

This passive way of thinking and participating is reflected in the fact that we often think our worship services are boring, unexciting, and even dead. Or when we talk about what we got or did not get out of the service, as if things are simply happening *to* us instead of *by* us. That too betrays a passive mentality.

So we need to be critical of ourselves, too. That is why we believe this subject is worth pursuing further.


## A Vital Role


We begin by facing that criticism we mentioned in the introduction: that the believer in the traditional type of worship service does not have an active role. We want to assert over against this that the believer *does* have an active role, even a vital role.

The argument is that because the pastor and elders lead the services and do most of the external, visible acts of worship, they are the only truly active ones in worship. And along with that, because the persons in the pew do not lead or perform most of the outward acts, they are not active in worship.

There are several reasons why this is wrong thinking.

First, the implication is simply wrong. Just because someone else leads in an activity does not mean the ones being led are not active and participating. That would be similar to arguing that because a teacher leads the students in learning, the students are not active in the classroom. Or that because a father leads in family devotions at home, the rest of the family is not active and participating. You sense the weakness, even silliness, of such an argument.

There are good reasons why the pastor and elders lead us in worship. They are the ones called by God to do this; this is part of their office. They are to oversee the public worship of God and to lead the congregation in the various elements of the service. God does not give this calling to any and every member of the congregation.

Specifically, the pastor is given the authority to lead the service because he is given the right to speak on God's behalf to the people, in the salutation and benediction, as well as in the preaching of the Word. Again, the believer is not given this authority in the worship service.

Besides, to have the elders leading the worship service is doing all things in decency and in order, as the Scripture directs in 1 Cor. 14:40, "Let all things be done decently and in order." The service can quickly become a chaotic circus if all kinds of people are leading the worship. That is, in fact, what has happened in many Reformed and Evangelical churches today. As a parade of people go up and down the aisles and the platform of the sanctuary, the fear of God is lost and the worship of God is minimized.

Having the pastor and elders lead the worship services also prevents other problems, such as members vying for control on worship teams, or striving to gain a more visible role in the service, or trying to introduce unbiblical innovations into the worship of God.

To assert this position is not to say that the believers have no active role in the worship service. They certainly do. That is what has to be stressed at this point. That this is so is evident from several points of view.

In the first place, it is evident from the viewpoint of the believer's salvation. When God saves his elect, His purpose is to make them a worshiping people, a people for "the praise of the glory of his grace" (Eph. 1:6). And that is what his grace actually accomplishes (cf. Is. 43:21; 1 Pet. 2:9). How then could we not be active in worship if this is what God by his saving grace has made us and given us to be?

A. W. Tozer, in his great little book on worship, puts it this way, "Jesus was born of a virgin, suffered under Pontius Pilate, died on the cross and rose from the grave to make worshipers out of rebels! He has done it all through grace. We are the recipients."[1]

Therefore God gives his people an active role in worship, because this is the reason he has saved them. His grace makes them worshipers and enables them to worship him in spirit and in truth. And all of Scripture reveals that this is what the saved believer does: he worships God, actively, consciously, no matter his specific place in the service. If you stand in grace, you do and you must participate in the worship of God!

In fact, we may say that there cannot be worship apart from a worshiping people! Worship implies worshipers! That is how vital our role is in worship. It is important that we remember this truth. If we have lost sight of our role, let us look at our salvation! If we have fallen into a passive mindset with regard to our place in public worship, or are bored with our traditional style, let us look at the grace of God to us in Jesus Christ!

In the second place, that the child of God has a vital role in worship is evident from the viewpoint of what public worship is (the nature of worship). We have in mind here especially the relationship between worship and the doctrine of the covenant. There are two things we wish to bring out here.

For one thing, public worship is covenantal because it is the gathering together of the covenant people of God. Worship is a corporate affair because the people of God in the covenant of grace are a body, the body of Christ, the church. They are not individual worshipers, to worship by themselves and on their own. But by virtue of God's covenant they are formed into a corporate worshiping people. That is why we gather together for public worship.

---

1. A. W. Tozer, *Whatever Happened to Worship: A Call to True Worship* (Camp Hill, PA: Christian Publications, 1985), 11.

That means, then, that worship belongs to the whole congregation, not to just the adults in the congregation, not to
just the pastor and the elders. No, worship is the business of
the whole church: the office-bearers, the adult confessing
members, the young people and children who are baptized
members, these all participate.

That is one reason why we do not take the children out of
our services or have them come forward during the service
for "children's church." They are part of the worshiping congregation; they do participate! The same is true of our young
people. We do not have to have a special worship service led
by young people to have them become involved in worship or
to make them feel more involved. They are members of God's
covenant and therefore are part of the worshiping congregation! In every service, every member of the covenant of grace
is a worshiper, an active participant. That is the vital place
God gives to his people in worship.

For another thing (still in connection with the covenant of
grace), we must also keep in mind that worship is covenant
fellowship between God and his people in Jesus Christ. Or as
some have put it, it is covenantal dialogue between God and
his people.

That is, in our worship God comes to dwell with us and to
reveal his saving communion with us. He draws near to us as
our sovereign Friend and calls us to meet him as his friend-
servants; he walks and talks with us by his Spirit and Word.
And we draw near to him to walk with him and talk with him.
Worship is intimate, conscious, covenantal fellowship!

This fellowship shows the important place God gives to his
people in worship. The fellowship of the covenant is mutual;
it involves and must involve our activity. If we understand worship to be so, then you and I also know we are not and cannot be passive bystanders or observers. Things don't just
happen around us and to us; but we are engaged actively in
holy communion with God! If this is what worship is, how
could we just sit there and do nothing?! Or be weary and
bored?! Or think the service dead?!

In the third place, the believer's vital role in worship is also evident from all that the Scriptures say about worship and from the words that it uses to describe worship. In the Bible worship is not just a noun; it is a verb, and a transitive one at that. "To worship" is to be active and do something. The various words for worship in the Bible mean, "to bow down to," "to kiss the hand toward," "to serve," "to show fear to," "to honor and reverence," "to praise"—all activities!

Our English word *worship* means "to ascribe worth to," which implies active participation. The word *liturgy* does not refer simply to the form of worship and the layout of the elements, but it literally means "work of the people," again, pointing us to their vital role in worship.

From these three perspectives we see that God's people have a vital role in the worship of God. They are not passive spectators at all, but are most surely active participants.

# 9

# A Conscious Involvement

*Charles Terpstra*

———•·•·•———

GOD'S PEOPLE HAVE A VITAL ROLE IN THE WORSHIP OF God. We are not passive spectators but active participants.

That brings us to our second main point, in which we want to examine specifically our conscious involvement in worship. By looking at the worship service and its various elements, we want to show how we are active and how we must be active.

We return to the idea that the Reformed worship service is to be seen as covenant fellowship or dialogue between God and his people in Christ. Keeping this in mind, we can divide the service into those parts in which God speaks to us and those parts in which we respond and speak to God. Let us look at some of the specific elements of our service to see how this works out in terms of our activity.

## In Our Listening

God speaks to us, for example, in the salutation ("Grace, mercy, and peace...") and benediction ("The grace of our Lord Jesus Christ..."). We might be tempted to say that because we are silent when these things are being spoken to us, we are also passive. But such is not the case. This is the Word of greeting to us and the Word of parting to us from our covenant Father and Friend. And we must be active in hearing and receiving this Word! In this there is fellowship with the living God!

Are we passive when a friend is conversing with us? Do we act as if nothing is happening and let the words pass over us? Of course not! How much more then in the worship of God! Also in listening to God's speech we must be bowing down before him, serving him, reverencing him, and praising him.

The same is true of God's speech to us in the reading of the law and in the reading of Scripture. We would even say it is true of God's Word to us in the singing! In each case God is addressing his people covenantally. And we are to be active in receiving that Word of our covenant God. Passive we must not be; hearing and receiving God's Word is the work of worship. And it is hard work; it requires our conscious participation and strenuous effort.

Is it perhaps the case that because we have lost sight of this work and activity we can act bored and be sleepy and let our minds wander when God is speaking to us? Have we let our culture of entertainment so influence us that we come to the service not to work and think but to be entertained? Then let us remember to be conscious of what we must be doing when God is speaking to us as our covenant Friend.

## In Our Speaking

Furthermore, we are also to be consciously involved in the parts of worship where *we* are speaking *to God*. In the service we respond to God's speech by speaking to him. There is, for example, the doxology, the opening song of praise. By means of that song we are ascribing worth to God, telling him what we think of him, why we would bow down before him. We must be conscious of that and think about that and weigh our words concerning that. In other words, this may not be done passively, but actively.

The same is true of the rest of the songs we sing in the service, the psalms and the hymns. Singing is a highly spiritual activity. It may not be done in a thoughtless and careless manner. Yet we often do. But then let us remember that when we sing, our covenant God is speaking to us, as we said. And we must think on his speech.

But we are also responding to him and speaking to him as his friends. We are praising and extolling and adoring him, telling him of his greatness and his glory. Clearly, that means conscious involvement.

In the psalms we also speak out of the wide variety of our experiences in life and express our deepest feelings. We not only ascribe worth to God, but we confess sin and mourn; we cry out because of suffering and pain and sorrow; we complain on account of the persecution of enemies; we pray and ask God to do things for us. All of this implies conscious involvement. Do we not think about what we are saying to God in these things? Do we not feel with the psalmists?

Still more, in the worship service we pray. The congregational prayer is also part of our covenantal speech to God, and it requires conscious involvement. Yes, the pastor or elder leads in this prayer, but it is the congregation's prayer, and we must be making it with and through the pastor/elder. That means that when the pastor is praying, we are following along carefully, saying and pondering the words with him. This is not nap time, or time to go over our weekly calendar of activities. This is prayer time! We are conversing with our heavenly Father, and it is the work of worship.

So it is also in the giving of our offerings. When we present our gifts in the offertory, we are responding to God and speaking to him. We are expressing our thanks for his unspeakable gift of grace in Jesus Christ. We are thanking him for his love that makes us love the poor and needy and contribute to their support. We are praising him for the means he gives us to support his kingdom and cause in the world.

And again, all of this presupposes our conscious involvement. This activity must also be done with great thought and care and desire. The offertory is not a time to relieve ourselves, whether at the drinking fountain or in the bathroom.

It is not a time to take a break from the work of worship, so that we can think about what we want and do what we want. Also our giving is to be an act of worship. It is a time for meditating on the grace of God to us, for giving thanks and praise as our hand places money into the plate. Let us do this consciously!

## With Our Whole Being

We must not forget that these conscious acts of worship are to be performed in the godly attitudes that mark true worship. We must sing and pray and give and listen in the fear of God, with genuine thanksgiving, in true love for God and our fellow saints, and in real joy in the Lord. This is conscious involvement. Worship without these is worthless and vain; it is blasphemous.

We must remember that our active involvement in worship involves the whole person—heart, soul, and body. Our worship must come from the heart, our spiritual center. Our worship must involve our souls, i.e., our minds and our wills. There is thinking and willing to do, and they must be done. And our worship involves our bodies: our brains, our mouths, our hands, and our legs—really the whole of us. Let us see to it that the whole of us, from heart to head to feet, is engaged and working spiritually.

We have to realize that this kind of conscious involvement is the answer to the danger of formalism in our worship on the one hand and innovation on the other hand.

We use the same liturgy week after week. The form of our worship we believe is biblical and proper. But that does not mean we cannot fall into the sin of formalism, of using the right means of worship in the wrong way, just going through the motions, as if the elements were empty, insignificant rituals. What keeps us from this sin is conscious, spiritual involvement, engaging ourselves in the real work of worship. We must know our place and know what we are doing and know whom we are serving.

This conscious involvement is the answer to the danger of introducing innovations into the worship of God. Why is it that many in the modern church want liturgical change and new forms? Not because there was something wrong with the old forms of worship, with the traditional elements of the service, but because they themselves have lost the wonder of worship, have forgotten to be involved in the conscious activity of bowing before and fellowshipping with the God of heaven. The services of many churches are dead because the worshipers are spiritually dead! Maybe for us, as well.

The answer, then, is not a changing of the service and the elements, not the introduction of the latest fads for worship. But the answer is change in people's hearts and minds, change in the way they handle the traditional elements, such that they involve themselves consciously in worship through the biblical means established. That is what we need: change in our hearts. Change in the way we act in the worship of the great God of heaven and earth.

# 10

## A Serious Preparation for Worship

*Charles Terpstra*

———◆•◆•◆———

A FINAL AREA OF CONCERN AND CONSIDERATION IS THAT of *preparing* for worship.

If the worship of God is such a serious, solemn activity, then it must be entered into and carried out with careful *preparation*. Is it not true that if we have planned some important dinner-date with friends, then we take the necessary time and steps to get ready for it? How much more when we have an appointment with God in his house each Lord's day!

### Three Parts

There are three parts to our preparation for worship. We will start with the narrowest aspect and move to the broadest.

First, our preparation for worship must take place just before the service begins—that is, when we have come to the church building and are seated in the sanctuary prior to the start of the formal service. This is an important time in terms of preparing ourselves for what is to take place. We need to begin seeking God's face, waiting to meet him, to hear him, and to fellowship with him. Therefore we ought to be in prayer and meditation through the Word. Instead we often waste this time through frivolous activities. Let us be conscious of the need to prepare to meet our God (see Amos 4:12).

Second, our preparation for worship must begin even before we arrive at the church building. Sunday morning and evening at home before the service is a critical time also in terms of how ready we will be to worship the Lord. We all know how hurried and hassled we can be on Sunday morning. We sleep too late and become rushed. We fight for time in the shower and bathroom. We wolf down our breakfast. Maybe there is time for family devotions, maybe not. And then we rush out the door and hurry to church, arriving perhaps at the last minute, or with just enough time to read the bulletin. And do we expect to be ready to enter God's presence and worship him in spirit and in truth, with mind and body fully engaged?

We must work hard(er) at preparing for worship on Sunday morning and evening. We can do better, much better. We must give ourselves time to get all the mundane things done on time. But we must do so in order that we may also prepare our hearts for worship. Make and take time for personal or family devotions. Stop to read and pray and ask God's blessing on you and the pastor and the service. Coming in this way, we will surely be better prepared to glorify God and be edified ourselves.

And then third, our preparation for worship covers the time of the whole week. We really cannot worship properly on Sunday unless we are living the whole week in preparation for worshiping the Lord. What that means is that we must be living in the fear of God and in the service of God all week in order for us to have true worship on the Lord's day. We cannot fear and worship God on only one day. We cannot live in an ungodly manner all week, and then expect to come ready to bow before God and give him thanks and praise on Sunday. We cannot be living in blatant disobedience to the will of God during the week, and then expect to come and do obeisance to the Lord on Sunday. We cannot be defying God's Word Monday through Saturday, and then think we will be ready to hear his Word on Sunday.

No, we must be living before his face all week long, day in and day out. We must be striving to do his will. Our whole life is to be a sacrifice of thanks and praise to the Lord. "I beseech you therefore, brethren, by the mercies of God, that ye present your bodies a living sacrifice, holy, acceptable unto God, which is your reasonable service" (Romans 12:1). When it is, then we will also be prepared to enter the gates of worship and offer our sacrifice of thanks and praise there.

## Personal and Family Worship

There are a couple of specific things we wish to mention yet in connection with this activity of godly preparation during the week. This is what we usually call personal and family worship or devotions. This is a concrete way in which we can prepare our hearts and minds to worship on Sunday. If we are spending time daily with God through his Word and through prayer, then we are keeping ourselves in spiritual shape to work at worship on Sunday. Of course, it is true that the public worship of God on Sunday feeds and empowers our personal and family worship during the week, but the opposite is also true. And then it is certainly true that our time with God during the week makes us hungry and thirsty for God in the services on Sunday.

This weekly worship time is also critically important for our children. It is in our family worship that we instruct them in the basic principles of public worship. We teach the importance of drawing near to God in covenant fellowship, of hearing his Word, of calling on him in prayer, and perhaps singing also. We teach them the godly attitudes that must characterize all our worship: reverence, humility, submission, quietness, joy, and faith.

Thinking of these things makes us think that maybe we have touched on another reason why we do not worship the Lord as fully and acceptably and profitably as we ought; why our hearts are often cold and our service formalistic; why the service seems long and boring; why we would begin to clamor for something new and innovative in worship. It may be because we are not seeking God in private worship and in family worship. This is at least something each of us needs to think seriously about.

Van Dellen and Monsma, in their *Church Order Commentary,* make the following pertinent statement concerning this: "As spiritual life begins to wane, formalistic and extraordinary observances begin to increase. He who serves God in Spirit and with devotion will have little need for the unusual, and for constant innovations."[1]

As we come to the end of our subject, we trust this has made us realize anew the vital role we have in worship, how we must be consciously involved, and how we ought to prepare for such a holy activity. Having been reminded of these things, let us put them into practice diligently—for the betterment of our worship, and above all, for the glory of God.

---

1. Idzerd Van Dellen and Martin Monsma (Grand Rapids, Mich.: Zondervan Publishing House, 1941), 275.

# Contributors

————— •◦•◦• —————

BARRY GRITTERS (A.B., Calvin College, B.D., Protestant Reformed Theological Seminary, currently seeking Th.M., Calvin Theological Seminary) is professor of New Testament and Practical Theology at the Theological School of the Protestant Reformed Churches in Grandville, Michigan. After graduating from the Protestant Reformed Theological Seminary, he served two pastorates until 2003, when he accepted the churches' appointment to the Seminary. His other published works include *Public Worship and the Reformed Faith, Grace Uncommon, Antichrist,* and *The Family: Foundations are Shaking.*

DAVID J. ENGELSMA (A.B., Calvin College, B.D., Protestant Reformed Theological Seminary, Th.M., Calvin Theological Seminary) is professor of Dogmatics and Old Testament Studies at the Theological School of the Protestant Reformed Churches. He is also the current editor of the *Standard Bearer.* His other published works include *Hyper-Calvinism & the Call of the Gospel: An Examination of the "Well-Meant Offer" of the Gospel; Reformed Education: The Christian School as Demand of the Covenant; Marriage, the Mystery of Christ & the Church: The Covenant-Bond in Scripture and History; Christ's Spiritual Kingdom: A Defense of Reformed Amillennialism;* and *Common Grace Revisited: A Response to Richard J. Mouw's* He Shines in All That's Fair.

CHARLES TERPSTRA (attended Calvin College, B.D., Protestant Reformed Theological Seminary) is the pastor of First Protestant Reformed Church in Holland, Michigan. He has also served pastorates in Pella, Iowa and South Holland, Illinois. His other published work is entitled *The Reformation: A Return to the Primacy of the Preaching.*